Woodpiles

poems by

Robert Longoni

Moon Pony Press

1997

Acknowledgements

Thanks to the editors in whose publications these poems first appeared:

Mazagine: "Spring Morning," "Lacking Anything Swift," "To Vivian, From the High Country," "On the North Rim"
Earthcare: "Now a Lizard," "Walking into My Life Near Mount Baldy," "Why We Worship Light," "The View from Wasson Peak"
SandScript: "In My Twelfth Year"
Focus: "The Serbian Soldier"
Poetry of the Desert Southwest (anthology): "Intermission: For a Student Whose Brother Has Died"

Thanks to my special friends who helped shape this book with their insights and encouragement, most notably Meg Files, Louise Meyer, Barrie Ryan, Tom Speer, Ann Tousley, and Nancy Wall.

Parts of the descriptions of extended family members who are recognizable in these poems are fictionalized to better capture the spirit of their presence in my life.

Published by Moon Pony Press
Nard Taiz, editor
740 30th Ave., #78
Santa Cruz, CA 95062

Moon Pony Press is a non-profit division of the Pima College Foundation, Tucson, AZ, the publication of this book funded through the Christopher Taiz Memorial Fellowship.

Set in 11 on 12 Palatino
Lithography by Paper Mill Printers, Soquel, CA 95073

ISBN 0-934910-04-9

Contents

Cover from a watercolor by Lee Taiz

For the family of my early years,
a time of enchantment,
and for my present family,
who nurture me still.

Nothing less than the universe is beautiful.
—Simone Weil

Woodpiles: A Birthday Reflection

1

On this mild winter morning,
as my hair thins
toward the silky whiteness
of my father's
in his final days,
I calculate my age
to be the same as his
when, for the last time
before arthritis and willful debt
moved us West, he ordered me
to rearrange the woodpile.
"Ambition," he would say,
"show some ambition"
(like his father, I recall,
who tinkered with watches
for a second living
from the day he left the factory
till his eyes gave out),
and I would fall upon the scraps of wood,
fragments of his efforts
to furnish our lives
against a tide of vices —
studs, planks, bulk of beams,
blocks, squares in ply,
rectangles, the occasional maverick
diagonal cut or a dowel —
until, one with my labor,
I learned the necessary art:
to displace as little air
as possible, forging space
for things whole,
constructing of scraps
and the motion of my hands
a replica of my will.

2

It was my mother's father,
a balding immigrant
with a wide lap for children,
content with a hoe
and what his own hands
could harvest on three continents,
who willed me his disposition,
a secret discipline
to whittle at a task
and never be satisfied,
and the patience
for dissolving seams
so that faced with rubble
or with ragged syllables,
I was resolved
to set all life in order,
to make every word
a note in a blessing.

But I lack his heroic heart,
and resolution fails me
when I need it most.
Like my father I am defined,
in spite of all,
by what is done
what is yet to be done
and what will never be.

3

Today as I sample misfortunes
like powdered chalk on my fingers
ambition returns, uninvited,
with the exotic sharpness,
almost the thrill,
of a broken milk bottle
slicing my right knee
under the waves of Narragansett,
leaving a wide scar
to surprise me each day
undressing:
seadrab flesh parted
into the same shy smile
my mother wore on her calf.

But how can ambition
in a timid heart
surpass what will never be?

4

My father could repent.
His desperate gestures
were never enough
to rebuild the ruins
of a fierce existence,
yet they spoke for something
in another language.

After the surgery
he waited for me
under the yellow mound
of his body, listening
for a closing note,
and I, who that morning
in a room streaming with sunshine
had pressed his hand
without bending for a kiss,
could say nothing —
held back
at the distance of a doorway
by a weakness
stronger than love.

5

Tell me, Father,
what did I withhold?
Did my hesitation
collapse a monument
you were beginning to construct
from a few scraps
of purpose?

Have we both learned,
finally, that ambition
does not smile back,
that only by rescuing
the splintered details
of our lives can we
build what is sufficient —
an edifice of sorts,
a foundation?

In My Twelfth Year

That winter
golden koi exploded
like fragments of sun
under the sweep of our blades

In the spring swell
some of them slipped the weir
on the neighbors' pond
and plopped into our brook
where they ruled

hammers of flame

Our Neighbors' Famous Barn

We had some neighbors
who converted their barn
into a nightclub
that made the papers
in other towns
but remained anonymous
on our landscape
until it burned
down to its slab
in the cold of winter.

It was a rosy night.
Revelers in pink
danced on our walls.
We mixed our faces
with the palpitating curtains,
watching the snow leap
with bare shadows of elms
as our neighbors' club
grew famous in our town.

Snakebit

By the seventh grade
he was gangly,
easygoing, not warm
but never mean.
His knees pumped
above the handlebars
and when he played ball,
his legs continued
into right field
while his torso
swung toward second.
He wasn't slow
but he made mistakes

in judgment. When
he asked the barber
for a pineapple,
expecting a crewcut,
the hair came off
down to the sheen
on the skull,
so he wore a cap
in school until,
asked to take it off,
he stood, doffed it
with a grand gesture,
and bravely grinned.

He never had a chance
to practice smirking
behind the wheel
at the indifference
of adults. Today
I can't even recall
whether his hair grew back
before he left
to visit relatives
in Florida, to make
whatever gesture he
had time to make
in their passenger seat.

Spring Morning

A burst of cactus wrens in the hollow
by the road. A whipsnake — stark black,
thick as my middle finger — glides
over gravel toward the house,
and a roadrunner, flashing blue,
beats his way from clothesline to roof.
For forty-six years I have been awkward.
Now something I have been trying to say
for months breaks its winter sleep
and reaches me like the smell of
last night's rain: *Today I am here*
where I belong. I have no task.
My lungs absorb the nearest mountains,
exchanging moisture with the evening sky.

Why We Worship Light

Wait for a certain summer morning
or a winter afternoon when you
don't notice the temperature
because it matches your body's
need for heat. The air doesn't
brighten but reveals what
you want revealed, clarifies.
You can count the spikes on ocotillos
and the branchings of palo verdes
on the neighboring slope,
and you can isolate saguaros
marching up the sides of hills
beyond the last houses. You
no longer wish for things
to be clearer than they are.

The View From Wasson Peak

We choose the near approach
the one without a trail
forgetting that scaling a mountain,
even a desert peak between valleys,
is seldom a straight climb.
Mostly we ascend in dry streambeds
or across a scruffy face
in search of a crack, a way in,
an easy way up, or at the base of
outcroppings we can't see over —
beyond each not the expected summit
but an intervening peak floating into view
and then another, several more.
Our feet contend with rock
that slides away, and hands
grasp at the wrong things:
roots and tufts of brittle grass.

At last the final lift,
a balance in the shoulders,
the brown level path.
The wind circles our knees
like a tired hound.
On the valley floor
highways run as straight
as men's wills until they collide
with the broad base of this range,
where they curl around crumbling hope
like tan fingers dying.

Portraits

My mother's father
although he was shy
never wore a hat
to hide his baldness
and carried his belly
with grace
like a favorite child.
Twenty years removed
from the hills of Tuscany
he stood with a hoe
in a field of cucumbers
and held to that hoe
all his years
except to make exchanges
for a child's laugh.

I strain to remember
his broken immigrant voice
but sometimes I think
it is he who dreams my dreams
and releases me at dawn
to the strangeness of a world
that was willed to me
by another ancestor
a tall mustachioed lieutenant
preserved in my father's parlor
whose singular wisdom
whenever I crossed his gaze
was to remain silent.

Matriarch

She cooks and tends her dahlias,
keeps house and consoles.
She watches others die —
her father, her mother,
a neighbor's child who drowns,
her husband, and a rebellious son

who argued, "A merciful God
would have us all die
in the same instant.
Death is not what we fear
but loss."

"That was not blasphemy,"
she assures her grieving daughters,
"there is no foolishness
in pain," and reopens her house
to all who need consolation.

Of her survivors
she requires only
that they admit sunlight
to shape its own memorial
among shadows where
she offers her body repose
until, recognizing the hour,
she spreads her hair
across two pillows

as if they were rocks
on the bank of a river.

Cattle in Winter

What they dream
and what they see
are the same —

slant of snow,
the sun in retreat,
drooping pines.

They stand
in the center of everything
like granite

sinking
sinking into themselves,
chewing on silence.

At Pasture

To this land
they brought
the smell of Spain
and oversized hearts
for roaming the same
burning earth.

When they galloped
through our wars
they learned
to let go
what flowed
on either side.

Now they release the past
with quivering flanks,
our fate no longer
fixed
on their forehead
like a star.

Now a Lizard

A lizard doing pushups
on the porch —
three, four pumps —
lofting his head
with the jerky motion
of a movie dinosaur.

A lizard so little
I could step on him unaware.
Our dog doesn't notice.
The lizard stays,
he is drooping,
he lingers in my view. . .

I watch in the certainty
of being spoken to
in a language
I don't understand,

as I've watched blackbirds
on cloudless afternoons
flickering in vines,
reading my eyes,

an egret on a bough
above cattails,
his eye like the eye
in a photograph,

or mudsnakes
flipped on the bank,
the fury of their plaid bellies.
In the water glaring back.

Now a lizard
waits out the morning
at the edge of the house's shadow —
a silhouette bowed,
brooding with sadness
more than his own.

I turn to these words
falling like magic
on the page, as if
themselves they were objects,
as if there were something
they could explain.

Lacking Anything Swift

Today a whitewinged dove
collided with the dining room window,
left a spray of pale yellow
on the tinted pane.
He lay stunned a long while —
he must have been flying at full speed
when he confused the reflected scene
with his future. His crop
had burst; tiny black seeds
clung to breast feathers.
He was as handsome as any pigeon.

We wanted to forgive him
his most human mistake,
hose down the glass,
wipe his feathers clean,
see him off.
But his eyes were opaque
and after long minutes
he couldn't move.
On the telephone
we were advised
to use a shovel,
lacking anything swift.

When he veered off, flapping,
in the middle of our chores,
he hardly cleared the greasewood.
But he had recovered enough
to grow alert, command his pain;
we could hope for more.
If not, most people hereabout
have dogs, and after dark
coyotes roam the hollows in packs.

Gallup in Summer Light

In front of Safeway descending rays
spray sunsets of fool's gold on turquoise.
Gray-faced silhouettes of the recently young
gather and nod, as if deciding
which glimmering mesa will mark home
when the last shard of light
has entered asphalt.

One of them approaches, long-faced,
in shapeless gabardine and faded plaid.
He calls me *brother* — self-trained salesman
like another, almost athletic, with quick eyes,
whose lips gave way to *sir* beside a liquor store,
the roadside hills still neon with dawn.

I search for a gesture, imagine my foolish
fat anglo face bleating *yes* and *yes*
and *yes*, a flash of stiff dollars
bribing me into their joyless circle,
my overfed lips, cracked with adobe dust,
addressing their women
whose bodies will cave in
beyond the circle of mustard-faced bluffs —

still deaf to voices rehearsing within me
like drumbeats to a forgotten dance:

> *You are Navajo, of the Diné, the people*
> *who read landscapes like scripture.*
> *I have heard your children*
> *squealing in laundromats, round faces*
> *bright with orange and blue mornings.*
> *I have sat, gestureless and opaque,*
> *under village rims, watching them —*
> *arches flexed into rainbows —*
> *leap fissures that widen like secrets*
> *in the ceramic silence.*

The Serbian Soldier
   The Interview and the Interview Unspoken

Perhaps they would kill me
he said *if I refused,*
but he was already faceless
describing how he passed along
the sixteen-year-old
like a hand-me-down doll
to his comrades,
and when asked
Why the women? irritated
at the disbelieving mind
too slow for simple logic:
Because they were chosen.
Can't you see? Because
pain he did not need to say
is a seed planted
like a hard rubber ball
growing with layers of hate.

When hate fathers a child,
the child becomes
his mother's pain,
so children become
their mothers and
the mothers their children
and the men fathers
only of hate,
leaving them free of it.

We have a prayer for this freedom.
It is something to celebrate.

> *Hail Virgin*
> *Mother of Pain*
> *Hatred forever*
> *Be thy name.*

You must tell me when
this interview has ended
because I need to rest.
I am weary from defending
the cause of freedom,
which he did not think to say
is the same
as the work of creation.

Rescuing History Near the Freeway
A Wish for the Millennium

The descendants of history
will go to sleep
thinking they are victims
with stories of infamy
calcified in their hearts
and dream them off
one by one —
tales of demagogues
and hucksters,
panderers and thieves,
celebrations of emperors,
conquerors, assassins,
and smiling
smotherers of dreams.

They will wake to a vision
of their own deeds
in the company of the sun,
but they will find him,
the father of history,
without pride, storyless,
compelled to continue
visiting this sad world
because, wrongly exalted himself,
he knows less of life
than a filament of weed
in a parking lot

and has to borrow
what he knows of death
from a child
presenting her layered
flesh to the breeze
near the shadow of an overpass.

Intermission: For a Student Whose Brother Has Died

I step out of Ginsberg's belly song
into a corner of the night. Something
is awake in the dark — a flaking eucalyptus
at my back is breathing to itself;
palo verde dust, escaping neonyellow
provinces of the street, begins a
long sifting toward the tightskinned moon.
I received your note. You are excused
from next week's classes, you are commended
to the breathings of this alchemical night.

We Stop Our Walk

We stop our walk,
stand parallel to trees.
Our eyes drop
from the canopy
to the underbrush
at our knees
to the humid forest
floor. Our hearts,
stretched by middle age,
grow supple.
I wonder which of us
brought the other here.
It's my birthplace
that we're near
but you too
grew up by woods.

We stop walking
wordless, as if we've
done just this before.
When you touch me
I remember ripe gladioli
creaking with juice
in a moist cellar.
The order in the landscape
behind you is clear.
I see roots everywhere.

Helping the Soft Air
    On the Ferry, Wood's Hole to Martha's Vineyard

The first gulls glide
out of the morning fog
like weeping ghosts
to catch the updraft
behind the clumsy ship.
They flap into position,
flutter for a second,
float, adjust, then hang,
clean white and gray.
Their yellow eyes hold
in the whirl of wind.

I think of a slight boy,
always ten, posing with oars
near the top of his stroke,
of my own childhood fear
of dragonflies, said to stitch
at every open thing,
that made us bite our lips inside.
Soon I am leaning
with hundreds of strangers
to counter the drifting weight
of every loss we can remember
until the heavybodied steamer,
its husky voice, centers us all.
Together we help the soft air
enter the soft water.

In this seamless world
the gray island sails by.
Before we enter the slip
I watch a thick man
with red hair and white beard
rowing his fragile boat,
knowing when to lift an oar
and drift, adjusting.
I face the shore, dreaming
that we have already exchanged
our failures and that we honor
with our silence those who say nothing.

To My Mother
    Velia Grassi Longoni (1908-1988)

1

Were they true, the stories
you told us as children,
that before you were seven
you were buried alive
with sleeping sickness,
were rescued from a viper in your crib,
and sailed with your family
on the only steamer
that evaded the U-boats
from Buenos Aires to New York?
Was that really you, our timid mother,
or was it a florid imagination
that you hid so well,
along with your intelligence
and everything you longed for,
behind a balanced apron
and a tilted smile?
Is that why they called you Elsa,
those who knew you then —
as if there were two of you,
but only one that I could ever know?

You, the child who became our mother,
wandered for three years
in a jungle of alien words
until you walked home one day
with its fragrance on your hands.
After you left school behind
for your family, and left family
for family, how much of you
died every day — you who never
allowed yourself the pleasure
of a book and refused
to render a word on paper
until you could spell every syllable
and feel the contours on your tongue,
just as in the flower shop
you fondled each arriving bloom
and drowned in its aroma,
then learned its name
like a second flower.

2

Now that years have grown over
the person you became,
you live again for me
as you always were,
timid and loving and brave,
your memory settling familiar on my life
as I turn toward my beginnings
before my last days.

3

You are the part of me
that shrinks from the dark
corners of a lovely world.
Together we suffer,
bewildered by cruelty,
but we never condemn.
We leave splinters of ourselves
in everything we touch.

You are the reason I still hum
"Amapola" and "Ciribiribin,"
I savor polenta and
spaghetti with garlic and butter,
I fear the telephone,
I can't part with a scrap of paper
or release my children
to their splendid lives
and their ultimate dust.

Because of you
I cannot love with abandon,
but I love often
beyond the limits of fear
in a world without heroes,
more than reasonably happy

as I follow my breath
through silent regions
where you suffered alone.

Clouds Above Hawley Lake

From a snack bar at the Apache resort
after a morning adrift in the sun
we watch the clouds sail in over the tops
of ponderosas. We ignore the menu,
pretend a conversation with the cook,
a retired Kansan, an authority on frybread
who now declares the summer storms on time.
Shadows darken the lake, then
swallow the path to our campground.
By the time we step outdoors
the clouds, low and thick,
have made a province of our lives.

We call home in a cloudburst
from a booth on a muddy slope,
watching the last of the rowboats
swing to a thud at the dock.
Abandoning plans for firewood,
we drive glowing backroads in search
of streams that feed this lake.
We remind ourselves to memorize
the rhythms of the afternoon storms.

Tomorrow we will wind to the top
of a peak that commands this high
basin, where we will look down
on our present existence with
the attentiveness of rainclouds.

To Vivian, From the High Country

The pines here, while their crowns
track the sun, are present to each other.
We who flash through their sacred caves
are only what they imagine.

Summer storms residing on the great peaks
rumble over forests and lakes
before crashing through our camp.
How long it rains, and how hard,
decides our day. Other times,
other places — even you —
are as distant as dreams.

Lying alone in the back of a pickup
on the deepest of forest nights
I hold your face before my eyes.
I try to make my will strong.
It's not the dark — I've always
feared the dark — it's knowing
how easy it will be for all this
to go on without me.

Walking into My Life Near Mount Baldy

The Little Colorado sliding
off both shoulders of Baldy,
undulating meadows at 9,000 feet,
forests draping knolls, crowding
the high reaches of peaks —
this whole landscape
pressed against the sky
has been inside me.

On the edge of a tilted pasture
the slender East Fork
pushes through crowds of fleabane,
bends on itself, forgets its way.
The West Fork glides through Sheep Crossing,
plunges through logjams
toward their junction at Greer.
Together they will cross the vast plateau
that dries up in the north
to join the muddy dredging
of the Colorado a mile below
the earth's crust.

        I vanish
from the silent company of Herefords,
rise to groves of aspen and spruce,
circle towering columns
of rock, level off in the woods,
moss and fern under foot,
ascend again rapidly,
breath parceled out.

From a lookout I see the gray
outlines of the Blue Range,
Big Lake like a fragment
of sky on the distant floor,
and before me — a memory awaking —
the long slope of Baldy.
A pair of eagles
sailing from a peak
above the spears of trees
circle outcroppings, soar
between and through clouds,
hanging, joining and sliding apart,
plunging.

        I breathe the communal air,
then descend like everything else
falling away from the sacred mountain.

On the North Rim

After the red cliffs
everything tasseled
and fluffed
slumbers in meadows

Ponderosas rot
like centipedes
A few slide
unseen into canyons

Somewhere below
an agave burns
in the ether of
its own will

Returning
>Near Ramah Lake, Zuni Mountains, New Mexico

In the bright morning flood
peregrine shadows whirl
high on the brow
of slumbering rock,
spirits of trees
that have dreamed themselves
brilliantly into stone
rise from shallow washes
toward the sheen of raven,
the hawk's floating arc.

>We who come here
>delivered of our promises
>return
>to our own beginnings.

Ancestral travelers
without names
lie unsplintered
in turquoise
between pink fingers
of cliffs.

>The selves
>we have not dreamed
>wait unpostured
>like rooms beside the sea
>while the light
>arranges itself
>inside the threshold.

Mule deer chew
within the outlines
of oak leaves.
A porcupine on a ridge
that slopes into shadow
carries a meadow of sunlight
fibered on his back.

>Everything is incomplete
>except the lines.
>Without words they
>seek their own solutions.
>They make room
>for the horizon,
>which has not
>thought to enter.

In Duet

> *It's the human voice*
> *that we're trying to imitate.*
> —Miriam Fried

When a violinist
on the radio
declares her secret, I
am suddenly wise
about music.
Though I can't play a note,
I know the score.
I recognize the trumpet
in the tenor's wail
and feel a trombone
sliding down my throat.

You, on the other hand,
brushed by the oboe,
confuse it with
my shy body.
A cello moans
from your ribs.
Our lungs and heart
in duet
stretch to the
tautness of drums.
The pendulous moon
is of our making now.
Bassoons well up
between our toes.
A measured bass
steadies
the sliding sand.

Driving West with Vivian in October,
Near the Mogollon Rim

> *. . . what the Spaniards had called the despoblado,*
> *the howling wilderness. . . consisted of a*
> *hundred-mile stretch of mountains culminating in*
> *the thousand-foot wall of the Rim itself, and a*
> *fifty-mile stretch of harsh desert beyond the Rim.*
> —Douglas Preston, *Cities of Gold*

1

Ponderosas drop long shadows
like spent weapons on the pavement —
rows of collapsing monuments
to Coronado and his troops
where they crawled
out of the lower *despoblado,*
completing a cycle from hope
to despair to hope
before they crucified hope
on a Zuni cross.

You drive on through,
I close my eyes.
We are joined in the present,
surviving more
than what they left behind
who changed nothing
except the way
we count our miseries.

Yet my thoughts slide
away from you
down over the rim
through serene layers of purple
to Pleasant Valley,
where only a century ago
generations of ranchers
named Tewksbury and Graham
picked each other off their horses,
and the Committee of Fifty
finished the work without a thought
to the King of Spain,
the salvation of souls,
or the residue of loss
in the eyes of strangers
gliding above afternoon haze.

2

You continue driving
on the edges of the day.
I search for faces
that preserve the landscape
in a remembered world,
but all is merged
in a flash of pavement
with legions of men and women
sagging from crosses,
featureless
against the narrow light,
and when I listen for the breath
of communal voices,
a wilderness grown
wider than the colossal
imaginings of conquerors
answers with howling
from Auschwitz and Sarajevo
Hiroshima and My Lai
Gettysburg and Wounded Knee.

$\longrightarrow$

3

Restored to your side,
I watch the oldest trees
outscale the afternoon,
grow round-topped, fluted,
pushing open their crowns
to merge with the planet's light.
Limbs underneath hang black,
waiting to drop,
to bounce off asphalt
or crack on soil
where they will soften
for seeds, hold off
the cold, quiet the
pavement's indifferent hum.
How much light can they absorb,
those ponderous souls,
by turning themselves inside out?
How much stretching
before a hint of radiance
reaches a fallen cone?

I drowse in memory.
The bodies I choose to dream
glide across ties
on trestles of childhood —
slender brown fingers
on measured notes
of an endless song
above a glancing river. . .
until the sun slashes again
from the other side of
everything familiar,
pitches solitary thoughts
over rows of torsos
spaced like harp strings,
vibrates fears
in receding daylight
till they merge
with the fragrance
of ungainly pines
migrating, reaching
through dusk, wrapping us,
our pitiful shells,
in their shadows.

On a Mountain Trail, After Fifty

With his earliest wish
he befriended mountains,
led there by the faces
of grasshoppers
who knew something
they hid in their wings.

Trailing ferns now,
circling crags and spiraling
spruce, he is surprised
by the familiar
as if still walking
with childhood friends:

Howie, shy at ten,
high cranium balanced
like a boulder
near the trail,
Thelma in paisley
brushed by light.

In a luminous meadow
as vivid and cool
as memory, secure as
a planet without war,
he releases his lingering dreams.
A drumroll of thunder

floats over layered ridges
he will never reach
except in his thoughts
swelling by the trail
toward a cataract
of multiplying voices.

Grasshoppers understood
in the blaze of yesterday,
with no need to remember
with nothing to forget,
whichever way they flew
that way was

home: Howie and Thelma.
A spiral path to silence.
The sufficiency of thunder.

At 7:00 a.m., After a Night of Rain

My mother-in-law sits
hunched before the picture window,
sinking into her weight.
She is nearly eighty,
and this morning she delights in a chipmunk
who fumbles a piñon cone
off the end of a branch.
The universe, with this
small generous act,
withholds the question
that awaits her every morning,
today behind a pink shroud
absorbing the sunrise
under stolid cliffs.

I watch her from the loft,
feeling my shoulders
sag toward my chest.
One day soon, while I am
still learning a way to begin,
the shaggy ponderosas on the skyline
will diminish to green fuzz.
Then I will seek out
the soul of a hummingbird
to hold a moment steady
and yellow while forests,
rebounding, improvise jays,
and resurrected cliffs
vibrate with morning.

Cross Words in a Hospital Room

1

Herman in the next bed after his third surgery
grouses all day, shoves at trays of prepared food,
shuns a liquid diet, refuses to get up and urinate
until he yellows the pillowcase and splashes the peach walls.
He tugs at the IV buried in his purple right wrist,
yanks at the replacement in the other arm as if
extracting a tuberous weed-root from a bed of violets,
accuses every nurse who enters of concealing a needle
or a stouter probe for his bruised body — even the plump
Iranian grandmother with the dyed-black upswept hair
who coos to him at midnight as she starts her rounds,
"How are you tonight, Honey? Are you more comfortable,
Sweetheart?" – and complains all afternoon to his wife,
ten years his senior (who responds with the uninhibited
laughter of a child), that the doctor who should be here
pronouncing him fit to go home is too busy with
someone else's surgery until the culprit himself,
awkward and courteous in pointed boots and bolo tie,
walks in at ten to six to release him. "Where are
you hiding the knife?" Herman snarls, then presents
his legs like two dry sticks so a blond orderly
with a bulldog smile can spin his torso from the ankles
before standing him up like an emaciated manikin to be dressed.

2

Awake in my clean sheets, sustained and kept continent
by three umbilicals, I watch. I have only one hunger,
for your rejected broth. Your testy words — all words —
hang in the afternoon light. They reopen the complicated
wonders of the living a syllable at a time. From the page
I learn a sty sound is *oink*, a Sutherland solo an *aria*.
The summer they sweat in Soissons is *été*; calculating snakes
are *adders*. I am lulled by *pimento* and *portulaca*;
chihuahua leaves me giddy. *Statice* stands out among words
like purple gashes in the gold-red symmetry of autumn bouquets.
After you leave, when the lights go out and the hall gossip
fades to a hum, I discover the familiar place where
Sweetheart intersects with *pain* and where *perfect* aligns
itself with *bruises. Innocence* and *friends* will attach
in either direction. It never did matter which of us forgot
to close the back of his gown on his afternoon walk.
When we return to our lives, words will again bring choices.
But the words you leave behind have joined a company,
still twirling above me, rehearsing names for the horizon.

At Year's End, Trying to Explain

There comes that moment
When what you are is what you will be
—Charles Wright

1

Clover and mist
warm visits from the morning sun
tiny capsules of breath
whirring around my knees
before the wild honey bees were
gone, minnows in the river
and striped heads poking
the silver membrane of ponds
before whole colonies
grazing pollen behind the sun
smothered slowly
like old men picking dumps
for clues to their own extinction.

We who survive,
granted an alternate future,
find reasons to celebrate
what is left behind, bend it
into the tortured beauty
we saw once in Picasso
and continue to hear
disguised in Mozart's horns,
as if to prolong the planet's memory
before the future itself
becomes a fossil in our hearts.

2

Today, as I squint
across our redwood deck
into a hanging sun,
I am reminded of wild bees,
and lamenting I think of you,
my children, how I stood by
on the rim of your lives
believing it would be easy for you
as it was for me
to walk through fields
confident of something
on the other side,
guiding you, I thought,
with little more than my will.
You must have noticed
my will in the world
amounts to nothing,
for I come to things slowly —
to fatherhood, my other callings,
the finality of extinction.

But always a straggler
beginning each morning
dazed by the sun,
slowly I learn everything:

> The earth will turn to close another void.
> There are no bystanders on this planet.
> The question of who I am remains unsettled.
> Love sustains, you have endured.

Bend close, I need your blessing
while there is time
to seek myself,
a child wandering
in that moment
when the wild bees churned
in delirious clover.

Robert Longoni grew up in New England and moved to the desert Southwest as a teenager. He taught at the University of Arizona, directed the University's Poetry Center, and then taught for 22 years at Pima Community College, where he has been named Faculty Emeritus. He began writing poems in his thirties and has been published in an anthology and small magazines. He and his wife, Vivian, live most of the year in the Zuni Mountains of New Mexico.